# Guess What!

## Workbook 3

### with Online Resources

**American English**

Lynne Marie Robertson

Series Editor: Lesley Koustaff

CAMBRIDGE
UNIVERSITY PRESS

**CAMBRIDGE**
UNIVERSITY PRESS & ASSESSMENT

Shaftesbury Road, Cambridge  CB2 8EA, United Kingdom

One Liberty Plaza, 20th Floor, New York, NY 10006, USA

477 Williamstown Road, Port Melbourne, VIC 3207, Australia

314–321, 3rd Floor, Plot 3, Splendor Forum, Jasola District Centre, New Delhi – 110025, India

103 Penang Road, #05–06/07, Visioncrest Commercial, Singapore 238467

Cambridge University Press & Assessment is a department of the University of Cambridge.

We share the University's mission to contribute to society through the pursuit of education, learning and research at the highest international levels of excellence.

www.cambridge.org
Information on this title: www.cambridge.org/9781107556867

© Cambridge University Press & Assessment 2016

First published 2016

40  39  38  37  36  35  34  33  32  31  30  29  28

Printed in Dubai by Oriental Press

*A catalogue record for this publication is available from the British Library*

ISBN 978-1-107-55686-7 Workbook with Online Resources Level 3
ISBN 978-1-107-55685-0 Student's Book Level 3
ISBN 978-1-107-55687-4 Teacher's Book with DVD Level 3
ISBN 978-1-107-55690-4 Class Audio CDs Level 3
ISBN 978-1-107-55692-8 Flashcards Level 3
ISBN 978-1-107-55693-5 Presentation Plus DVD-ROM Level 3
ISBN 978-1-107-55694-2 Teacher's Resource and Tests CD-ROM Levels 3–4

Additional resources for this publication at www.cambridge.org/guesswhatamericanenglish

# Contents

# Welcome

**1** **Look and write the names.**

> Anna  Lily  ~~Lucas~~  Max  Tom

1 _Lucas_
2 _____
3 _____
4 _____
5 _____

**2** **Look at activity 1. Read and write _true_ or _false_.**

1 Tom likes art.  _true_
2 Anna is ten.  _____
3 Max is Lucas's dog.  _____
4 Lily's favorite sport is soccer.  _____
5 Lucas's favorite color is red.  _____

 **My picture dictionary** ➔ **Go to page 84: Find and write the new words.**

**Read and match.**

1 What's your name?  a I'm nine years old.
2 How old are you?  b My favorite color is green.
3 What's your favorite color?  c My name's Bill.
4 Do you like dogs?  d Yes, I can.
5 Do you have a bike?  e Yes, I do.
6 Can you ride a horse?  f No, I don't.

  **Answer the questions. Then draw your picture.**

1 What's your name?

*My name is* _____

2 How old are you?

_____

3 Do you have a bike?

_____

4 What's your favorite color?

_____

_____

5 Do you like dogs?

_____

6 Can you play tennis?

_____

Grammar **5**

**5** (Think) **Write the months in order. Then answer the question. Use the letters in the boxes to complete the answer.**

1. J a n u a r y

2. F [ ] _ _ _ _ _ _

3. M _ _ _ _ _

4. A _ _ _ _

5. M _ _

6. J _ _ [ ]

7. J _ [ ] _

8. A _ _ _ _ _ _

9. S _ _ _ _ _ _ _ _

10. O _ [ ] _ _ _ _

11. N _ [ ] _ _ _ _

12. D _ _ _ _ _ _ _

**How many months are there?**

_ W _ _ _ _

**6** (About Me) **Answer the questions.**

1 What month is it?

It is _____

2 What's your favorite month?

_____

My picture dictionary → Go to page 84: Find and write the new words.

## Skills: *Writing*

**7** Read the email. Circle the answers to the questions.

Hello!
My name's Jill. I'm (eleven) years old. My birthday is in April.
I have one brother and one sister. I have a pet rabbit.
My favorite sport is basketball. What about you?
Jill ☺

1  How old are you?
2  When is your birthday?
3  Do you have any brothers or sisters?
4  Do you have a pet?
5  What's your favorite sport?

**8**  Look at activity 7. Answer the questions for you.

1  *I'm* _____

2  _____

3  _____

4  _____

5  _____

**9** (About Me) Write an email to a pen pal.

*Hello!* _____

*My name's* _____

_____

_____

_____

_____

**10**  Ask and answer with a friend.

How old are you?     I'm eleven years old.

## 11 Read and number in order.

**a**
Let's do the treasure hunt together!

Good idea.

**b**
Treasure Hunt.
Find 7 things in 7 days.
Text 123 to join.
A surprise at the end!

**c**
It's a cell phone!

And look at this!

**d**
Happy birthday, Lily!

Thanks, Tom. Thanks everyone for your presents!

1

**e**
What's this present?

I don't know.

Open it, Lily!

**f**
Dad, can we do this treasure hunt, please?

Yes, of course! It sounds fun.

123 – there!

## 12 Look at activity 11. Write *yes* or *no*.

1  It's Tom's birthday.　　　　　　　　　　　　　　　　*no*

2  The present is a cell phone.

3  The treasure hunt is to find 7 things in 5 days.

4  Lily's friends don't want to do the treasure hunt.

5  The treasure hunt sounds fun.

**13** **Read and check the sentences that show the value: work together.**

**1** Let's do the treasure hunt together. ✓   **2** Let's find my dog. ☐

**3** I like card games. ☐   **4** Good idea. ☐

**5** Let's clean up. ☐   **6** I'm playing basketball. ☐

**14** **Circle the words that sound like *snake*.**

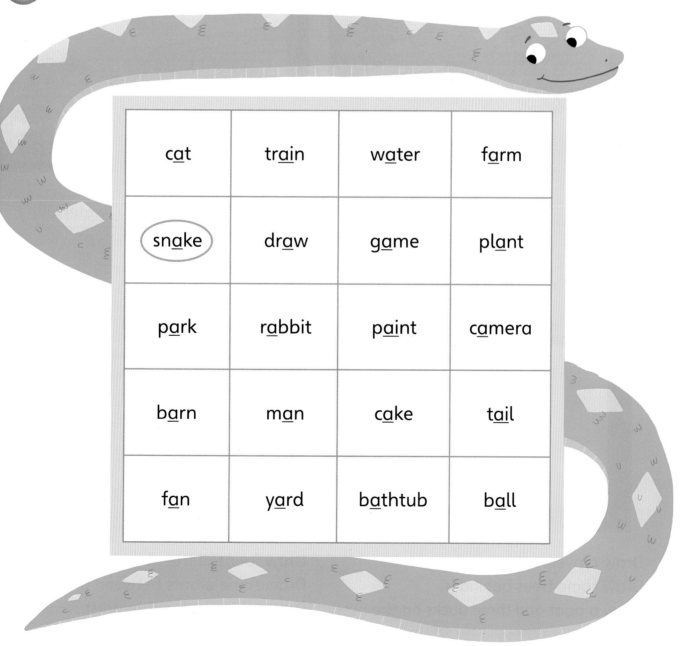

| | | | |
|---|---|---|---|
| c<u>a</u>t | tr<u>ai</u>n | w<u>a</u>ter | f<u>a</u>rm |
| (sn<u>a</u>ke) | dr<u>aw</u> | g<u>a</u>me | pl<u>a</u>nt |
| p<u>a</u>rk | r<u>a</u>bbit | p<u>ai</u>nt | c<u>a</u>mera |
| b<u>a</u>rn | m<u>a</u>n | c<u>a</u>ke | t<u>ai</u>l |
| f<u>a</u>n | y<u>a</u>rd | b<u>a</u>thtub | b<u>a</u>ll |

# What can you see in a landscape painting?

**1** **Look and match.**

birds  boat  forest  mountain

plants  river  ocean  waterfall

**2** **Draw two landscapes.**

**1**

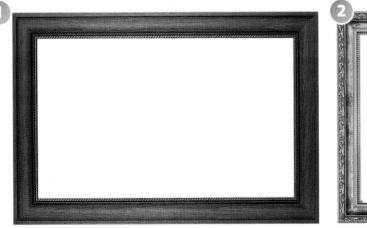

**2**

Draw a river.
Draw some trees behind it.
Draw a boat and three ducks on the river.

Draw four tall trees in a forest.
Draw some plants between the trees.
Draw an animal in the forest.

# Evaluation

## 1 Do the word puzzle.

**Down ↓**

 1

 2

 4

```
        1
        T
        O    4
     2  3 M
 5
```

**Across →**

3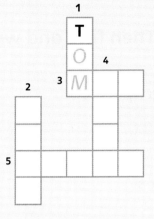

5

## 2 (About Me) Find and write the questions. Then answer.

1  are / old / you? / How

_How old are you?_

_I'm_ _____

2  your / When's / birthday?

_____

3  swim? / you / Can

_____

_____

4  color? / your / What's / favorite

_____

_____

5  you / Do / a / have / brother?

_____

_____

_____

## 3 (About Me) Complete the sentences about this unit.

1  I can talk about _____ .

2  I can write about _____ .

3  My favorite part is _____ .

## 4 (Puzzle) Guess what it is.

Go to page 93 and circle the answer.

11

**1** Look and guess. Then find and write the words.

1  llriarpaect

_caterpillar_

2  tubytfler

_____

3  sagrs

_____

4  relutt

_____

5  aisln

_____

6  eaginu gip

_____

7  refwol

_____

8  eret

_____

9  tribab

_____

10  fela

_____

**2**  Write the words from activity 1 on the lists.

| Animals | Plants |
|---|---|
| _caterpillar_ | _grass_ |
| | |
| | |
| | |
| | |

My picture dictionary ➡ Go to page 85: Find and write the new words.

**3** **Look and circle the words.**

**4** **Look and complete the sentences. Then color the animals.**

| ~~Her~~ Her His Our | big big ~~small~~ small |
|---|---|

**1**

_Her_ pet is _small_ and yellow.

**2**

_____ pet is _____ and gray.

**3**

_____ pet is _____ and brown.

**4**

_____ pet is _____ and orange.

**5** Look and circle the questions and answers.

1 (What's that?)
  What are those?

a (It's a snail.)
  They're snails.

2 What's that?
  What are those?

b It's a flower.
  They're flowers.

3 What's that?
  What are those?

c It's a turtle.
  They're turtles.

4 What's that?
  What are those?

d It's a bird.
  They're birds.

5 What's that?
  What are those?

e It's a leaf.
  They're leaves.

**6** Look and write the questions and answers.

| ~~butterflies~~ caterpillar spider trees |

1 What are those?
  They're butterflies.

2 What's that?
  _____
  _____

3 _____
  _____

4 _____
  _____

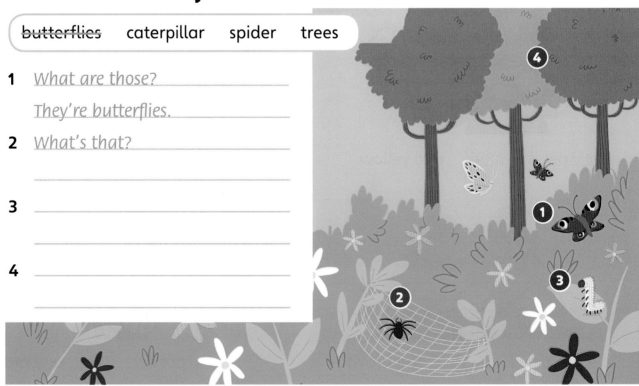

## Skills: *Writing*

**7** **Read the paragraph and write the words.**

> butterflies    leaves    ~~small~~    tree    white

My favorite bug is a caterpillar. Caterpillars are ¹___small___ . I like black and ²_____ caterpillars. You can see a caterpillar on a ³_____ . The caterpillar eats the green ⁴_____ . Beautiful ⁵_____ come from caterpillars.

**8** (About Me) **Answer the questions.**

**1** What's your favorite bug?

*My favorite bug is* _____

**2** What color is it?

_____

**3** Is it big or small or beautiful?

_____

**4** Where can you see it?

_____

**9** (About Me) **Write about your favorite bug.**

*My favorite bug* _____

_____

_____

_____

_____

_____

**10** (About Me) **Ask and answer with a friend.**

> What's your favorite animal?        My favorite animal is a horse.

**Read and match.**

| | |
|---|---|
| **1** Not now, Anna. | **2** Sorry, Anna. Thank you. |
| **3** Are those ears and a tail? | **4** Can we borrow it, please? |

**Look at activity 11. Answer the questions.**

1 What do they see behind the tree?    *Ears and a tail.*

2 What animal is behind the tree?    _____

3 What animal does Anna have?    _____

4 What can they do with it?    _____

5 Who is sorry?    _____

**16** Story

**13** **Look and write the questions and answers. Then check the picture that shows the value: respect and listen to others.**

~~Can I help?~~    Yes, you can. Thank you.    Can I help?    Not now.

**1**

Can I help?

**2**

**14** **Write the words with the same sound in the lists.**

~~cake~~    ~~tree~~    p<u>ai</u>nt    l<u>ea</u>f    m<u>a</u>ke    j<u>ea</u>ns
sl<u>ee</u>p    <u>ea</u>t    t<u>ai</u>l    chimpanz<u>ee</u>    tr<u>ai</u>n    sn<u>a</u>ke

**1**

cake

**2**

tree

# What types of habitats are there?

**1** Write the names of the habitats. Then circle the two correct sentences.

desert    grassland    ~~rain forest~~    tundra

rain forest

It's a hot place.
There are a lot of trees and leaves.
Lions live here.

It's a hot place.
Monkeys live here.
There is a lot of grass.

It's a cold place.
There are lots of trees.
Bears live here.

There is little water.
Snakes and spiders live here.
There are lots of fish.

**2**  Draw and write about a habitat in your country.

It's a _____ place. There are lots of _____ . _____ live here.

# Evaluation

**1** **Find and write the words.**

1  *What's that?*
   It's a flower.

2  _____
   They're leaves.

3  _____
   They're caterpillars.

4  _____
   It's a butterfly.

5  _____
   It's grass.

**2**  **Look and write the words.**

| My Your Our Their | ~~turtle~~ fish rabbit snail | ~~small~~ big white green |

_My_   _turtle_       _____  _____       _____  _____       _____  _____

is  _small_  .       is _____ .       is _____ .       is _____ .

**3**  **Complete the sentences about this unit.**

1  I can talk about _____ .

2  I can write about _____ .

3  My favorite part is _____ .

**4**  **Guess what it is.**

Go to page 93 and circle the answer.

**1** Look and number the picture.

1 playground
2 gym
3 science lab
4 sports field
5 cafeteria
6 art room
7 library
8 music room
9 reception
10 classroom

**2** (Think) Look at activity 1. Read the sentences and write the words.

1 You can paint pictures in this room          *art room*

2 There are desks and chairs in this room.

3 You can eat lunch in this room.

4 You have a science class in this room.

5 You can run, jump, and dance in this room.

6 You go here when you visit the school.

7 You can play soccer here.

8 You can play outside here.

9 You can read books here.

10 You can sing here.

My picture dictionary  Go to page 86: Find and write the new words.

**3** Look and circle the answers.

We're / (They're) on the sports field.

We're / They're in the art room.

We're / They're in the science lab.

We're / They're in the classroom.

**4** (Think) Look and complete the questions and answers.

1  Where are ___they___ ?  _____ at reception.

2  Where are _____ ?  ___We're___ in the library.

3  Where are _____ ?  _____ in the gym.

4  Where are _____ ?  _____ in the music room.

5  Where are _____ ?  _____ on the playground.

## 5 Read and match.

a They're playing basketball.

b They're playing soccer.

c We're playing basketball.

d We're playing soccer.

## 6 (Think) Look and write the questions and answers.

1 <u>What are you doing?</u>　　　　<u>We're playing ice hockey.</u>

2 <u>What are they doing?</u>　　　　<u>They're</u> _____

3 _____　　　　_____

4 _____　　　　_____

## Skills: *Writing*

**7** **Read the text. Circle the answers to the questions.**

My school is (small.) There are six classrooms, a library, and a big playground.

I like the library, but my favorite room is the gym. There are 18 children in my

classroom. My favorite class is English.

1   Is your school big or small?
2   What rooms and places are in your school?
3   What is your favorite room?
4   How many children are in your class?
5   What is your favorite class?

**8** (About Me) **Look at activity 7. Answer the questions.**

1   *My school is* _____

2   _____

3   _____

4   _____

5   _____

**9** **Write a description of your school.**

*My school* _____

_____

_____

_____

_____

_____

_____

**10** (About Me) **Ask and answer with a friend.**

What's your favorite class?        My favorite class is science.

## 11 Read and write the words.

Thank you!    pick up    ~~litter~~    Listen!

**a**

What are they doing?

They're picking up _litter_ . Let's help.

**b**

Hi, Aunt Pat. Can we help?

Yes, please. Can you _____ this litter?

**c**

Come on, Lily!

Wait! _____ What's that?

**d**

Thanks for your help! You can have the radio.

_____

## 12 Look at activity 11. Write *yes* or *no*.

1   Dad and Aunt Pat are in the gym.                          _no_

2   Aunt Pat is picking up litter.                           _____

3   The children don't help.                                 _____

4   Lily is listening to the radio.                          _____

5   Aunt Pat wants the radio.                                _____

**13** Look and check the pictures that show the value: keep your environment clean.

**14** Circle the words that sound like *tiger*.

# What materials can we recycle?

**1** **Look and match.**

**2** **Design two recycling bins for your school.**

Where is it? _____

Where is it? _____

What can children put in it? _____

What can children put in it? _____

# Evaluation

**1** **Look and answer the questions.**

**1** Where are the girls? *They're in the gym.*

**2** What are they doing? _____

**3** Where are the boys? _____

**4** What are they doing? _____

**5** Where are the teachers? _____

**6** What are they doing? _____

**7** Where are we? _____

**8** What are we doing? _____

**2**  **Complete the sentences about this unit.**

**1** I can talk about _____ .

**2** I can write about _____ .

**3** My favorite part is _____ .

**3**  **Guess what it is.**

Go to page 93 and circle the answer.

# Review Units 1 and 2

**1** Look and find the numbers. Answer the questions.

**1** Where are they? *They're in the science lab.*

**2** What are those? _____

**3** What's he doing? _____

**4** What are those? _____

**5** What are they doing? _____

**6** Where are they? _____

**7** What's that? _____

**8** What's that? _____

**2** (Think) Find 11 months ↓ →. Then answer the question.

```
N  O  V  E  M  B  E  R  T  J  S  F  G  M
A  C  B  Z  A  P  Y  E  J  U  N  E  K  A
W  T  A  Q  Y  N  A  C  I  L  T  B  O  R
B  O  N (J  A  N  U  A  R  Y) S  R  I  C
K  B  U  P  B  T  A  N  G  K  W  U  L  H
D  E  C  E  M  B  E  R  X  A  C  A  G  M
O  R  O  C  G  M  A  I  O  A  P  R  I  L
P  B  Y  A  U  G  U  S  T  W  B  Y  J  D
```

**One month is not in the puzzle. What month is it?**

**3** Look and write the questions.

1 _What's her name?_ It's Kate.
2 _____ It's in May.
3 _____ Her favorite color is pink.
4 _Who are they?_ They're my cousins.
5 _____ They're at the park.
6 _____ They're flying a kite.

**4** Look at the photographs in Activity 3. Complete the sentences.

1 _____His T-shirt_____ is yellow. 2 _____ is pink.
3 _____ are blue. 4 _____ is a plane.

**5** Think Answer the questions.

a bird   a butterfly   a caterpillar   a cafeteria
February   grass   a guinea pig   a library

1 These eat leaves. What are they? _a guinea pig_ and _____
2 You can eat here. Where is it? _____
3 You can read books here. Where is it? _____
4 These can fly. What are they? _____ and _____
5 This has 8 letters. What month is it? _____
6 This is a plant. What is it? _____

# School days

## 1 Write the days of the week.

|  | n a d y M o<br>_Monday_ | a u s d e T y<br>_____ | s d a y d e n W e<br>_____ |
|---|---|---|---|
| Sue | *(sheet music)* | *(pen and paintbrush)* | *(microscope and flask)* |
| Dan | *(microscope and flask)* | *(sneakers and jump rope)* | *(pen and paintbrush)* |

Dan    Sue

|  | y h r d u T s a<br>_____ | i a y F d r<br>_____ | y r t d S a a u<br>_____ | y S n d u a<br>_____ |
|---|---|---|---|---|
| Sue | *(math symbols)* | *(sneakers and jump rope)* | *(laptop)* | *(sheet music)* |
| Dan | *(sheet music)* | *(math symbols)* | *(soccer ball)* | *(laptop)* |

## 2 Look at activity 1. Write _yes_ or _no_.

1  She has math on Thursday. _____ _yes_
2  He has gym on Friday. _____
3  She has art on Monday. _____
4  He has soccer club on Saturday. _____
5  She has computer club on Sunday. _____

## 3 Look at activity 1. Write the sentences.

1  Monday: _She has music, and he has science._
2  Tuesday: _____
3  Wednesday: _____
4  Thursday: _____
5  Friday: _____

**My picture dictionary**  Go to page 87: Find and write the new words.

**4**  **Look and follow. Then complete the questions and answers.**

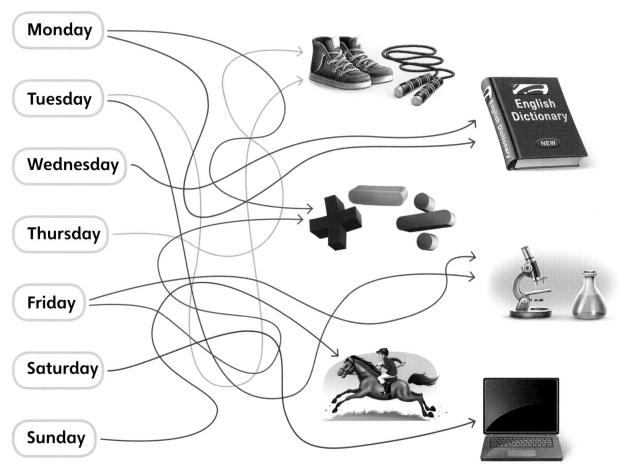

Monday
Tuesday
Wednesday
Thursday
Friday
Saturday
Sunday

1   Do we have gym on Thursday?                             *Yes, we do.*

2   Do we have English on Saturday?

3   Do we have math on Monday?

4   _____ science on Friday?

5   _____ computer club on Sunday?

6   _____ horseback riding club on Sunday?

**5** **Look at activity 4. Complete the sentences.**

1   _____*We don't have*_____ math on Thursday.

2   _____ English on Monday and Wednesday.

3   _____ science on Tuesday and Friday.

4   _____ horseback riding club on Thursday.

5   _____ computer club on Saturday.

6   _____ gym on Monday and Friday.

**6** **Read and complete Josh's day.**

Josh    Monica

**Tuesday**

**Monica**
Which classes do you have on Tuesday?

**Josh**
We have gym, science, and art in
the morning. Gym is before science.
Art is after science.

**Monica**
Which classes do you have in the afternoon?

**Josh**
We have English and math. We have English
after lunch. We have math after English.

**Monica**
Do you have a club after school?

**Josh**
Yes, I have soccer club in the evening.

*morning*
1 _____
2 _____ *science*
3 _____
*LUNCH*
*afternoon*
4 _____
5 _____
*evening*
6 _____

**7** **Look at activity 6. Write the answers.**

**1** Which class does Josh have after gym?

*He has science after gym.*

**2** Which class does Josh have after lunch?

**3** Which class does Josh have before lunch?

**4** Which class does Josh have before math?

**8** **Choose a day from your schedule. Answer the questions.**

**1** Which classes do you have in the morning?

**2** Which classes do you have in the afternoon?

**3** Do you have a club after school?

## Skills: *Writing*

**9** **Read the paragraph and write the words.**

> horseback   club   morning   ~~Saturday~~   music   competitions

My favorite day of the week is ¹ _Saturday_ . I have a ² _____
class in the ³ _____ . I have photography ⁴ _____ in the afternoon.
In the evening. I have a ⁵ _____ riding lesson and a dance
competition. I like ⁶ _____ .

**10** (About Me) **Answer the questions.**

1   What's your favorite day of the week?

_My favorite day is_ _____

2   What do you have in the morning?

_____

3   What do you have in the afternoon?

_____

4   What do you have in the evening?

_____

**11** (About Me) **Write about your favorite day.**

_My favorite_ _____

_____

_____

_____

_____

**12** (About Me) **Ask and answer with a friend.**

Do you have any clubs this week?

Yes, I have computer club on Thursday.

## 13 Read and number in order.

**a** It's very good, Tom.
What do you think, Max?

**b** We can't take a photograph of the painting.
What can we do now?
I have an idea!

**c** Is the art gallery open on Saturdays?
Yes, it is.
Come on. Let's go!

**d** Be careful!
Are you OK, Tom?
Yes, I'm fine. Don't worry.

**e** OK. Here we are.
Now where's the painting?
Over there!

**f** What day is it today?
Find this painting.
It's Saturday.
Great! I like art. Let's go to the art gallery.
1

## 14 Look at activity 13. Answer the questions.

1   Who likes art? _____Tom._____

2   What is open on Saturdays? _____

3   What can't they do? _____

4   What animal is in the painting? _____

5   What does Tom do? _____

**15** Look and check the pictures that show the value: be resourceful.

**16** Color the words that sound like *goat*. Then answer the question.

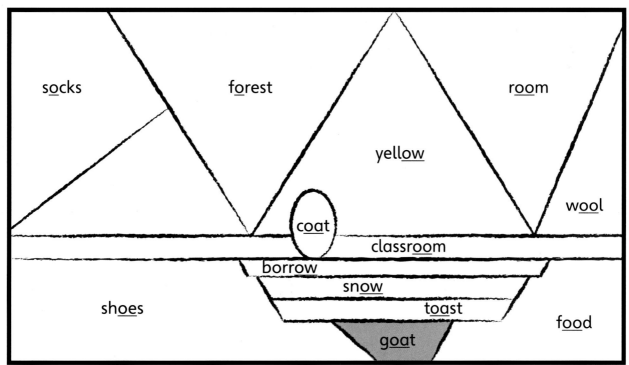

socks   forest   r<u>oo</u>m

yell<u>ow</u>

w<u>oo</u>l

c<u>oa</u>t

classr<u>oo</u>m

b<u>orrow</u>

sn<u>ow</u>

t<u>oa</u>st

sh<u>oe</u>s

f<u>oo</u>d

g<u>oa</u>t

What's in the picture? _____

# Which animals are nocturnal?

**1** **Read and check the sentences that are true for nocturnal animals.**

1 It finds food and eats at night. ✓

2 It likes running and flying in the day. ☐

3 It likes playing in the evening and at night. ☐

4 It sleeps in the morning and afternoon. ☐

**2** **Draw and label one animal in each box in the chart.**
**Then write sentences about each animal.**

|  | ✓ nocturnal | ✗ nocturnal |
|---|---|---|
| ✗ fly |  ❶ | ❷ |
| ✓ fly | ❸ | ❹ |

1  A scorpion is nocturnal. It can't fly. _____

2  _____

3  _____

4  _____

# Evaluation

 **Write the days of the week in the diary and answer the questions.**

Emily    Jacob

**Thursday**

10:00  art
2:00   English test
6:00   soccer club

**F**

9:00   gym
1:00   science

**Sa**

3:00   gym competition

**S**

10:00   photography club
12:00   lunch with Grandma

**1**  Do you have art on Friday?                          *No, we don't.*

**2**  Do you have art on Thursday?                        _____

**3**  Do you have a math test on Thursday?                _____

**4**  Do you have a gym competition on Saturday?          _____

 **Think** **Look at activity 1. Answer the questions about Emily.**

**1**  Look at Thursday. What does she have in the morning?    *She has art.*

**2**  Look at Thursday. What does she have in the evening?     _____

**3**  Look at Friday. What does she have in the morning?       _____

**4**  Look at Friday. What does she have in the afternoon?     _____

**5**  Look at Sunday. What does she have before lunch?         _____

 **About Me** **Complete the sentences about this unit.**

**1**  I can talk about _____ .

**2**  I can write about _____ .

**3**  My favorite part is _____ .

 **Puzzle** **Guess what it is.**

Go to page 93 and circle the answer.

37

# My day

**1** Look and write the answers.

> brush your teeth   get up   go to bed   ~~go to school~~
> have breakfast   have dinner   have lunch   take a shower

  go to school

**2** (About Me) Look at activity 1. Write six sentences about your day.

1  I _____get dressed_____ in the morning.

2  I _____

3  I _____ in the afternoon.

4  I _____ in the evening.

5  _____

6  _____

My picture dictionary  Go to page 88: Find and write the new words.

**3** **Read and match.**

1 I get dressed at seven o'clock.

2 I go to school at eight o'clock.

3 I eat lunch at twelve o'clock.

4 I go home at three thirty.

5 I eat dinner at seven thirty.

6 I go to bed at nine thirty.

**4** **Look and complete the sentences.**

1 I _____ get up _____ at _____ seven thirty _____ .

2 I _____ at _____ .

3 I _____ at _____ .

4 I _____ at _____ .

5 I _____ at _____ .

6 I _____ at _____ .

**5** (About Me) **Write sentences and draw the times.**

1 I _____ at _____ .

2 I _____ at _____ .

3 I _____ at _____ .

4 I _____ at _____ .

**6** **Think** **Read and answer the questions.**

Ken: What time do you get up?
Eva: I get up at seven thirty.
Ken: So do I.
Maya: I don't. I get up at seven o'clock.
Maya: What time do you go to bed?
Ken: I go to bed at nine o'clock.
Eva: I don't. I go to bed at eight thirty.
Maya: So do I.

Maya        Eva        Ken

1 Who gets up at seven o'clock?      _____Maya_____

2 Who gets up at seven thirty?      _____ and _____

3 Who goes to bed at eight thirty?      _____ and _____

4 Who goes to bed at nine o'clock?      _____

**7** **Look and complete the sentences.**

1      What time do you have dinner?

I ___have dinner___ at ___seven o'clock___ .

So do I.          I don't.

2      What time do you have breakfast?

I _____ at _____ .

I _____ at _____ .

**8** **About Me** **Ask and answer with two friends.**

I get up at …      So do I.      I don't. I get up at …

## Skills: *Writing*

**9** (About Me) **Write a questionnaire about a healthy lifestyle. Then ask a friend.**

~~have breakfast~~   play outside   ~~walk to school~~   ride a bike
~~get up~~   brush your teeth   watch TV   play sports
play computer games   drink orange juice

Yes / No

1  *Do you have breakfast every day?* _____  _____

2  *Do you walk to school in the morning?* _____  _____

3  *Do you like getting up early?* _____  _____

4  _____  _____

5  _____  _____

6  _____  _____

7  _____  _____

8  _____  _____

9  _____  _____

10 _____  _____

**10** (About Me) **Ask and answer with a friend.**

Do you have a healthy lifestyle?   Yes, I do. I walk to school every day.

## 11 Read and match.

> 1 I can do the race!
> 2 Thanks! Swimming is fun!
> 3 The first prize is a watch!
> 4 And the winner is … Lucas!

## 12 Look at activity 11. Circle the answers.

1  Lucas does _____ .
   **a** a swimming club    **b** a swimming race    **c** the first prize

2  Lucas thinks swimming is _____ .
   **a** fun    **b** great    **c** nice

3  Lucas wins _____ .
   **a** a present    **b** a test    **c** a prize

4  The prize is _____ .
   **a** a watch    **b** a race    **c** swimming lessons

**Check the activities that show the value: exercise.**

**1** do a bike race ✓     **2** go to baseball club ☐

**3** take a math test ☐     **4** play in a tennis competition ☐

**5** go to bed early ☐     **6** go roller-skating ☐

**7** take a shower ☐     **8** play sports after school ☐

 **Circle the words that sound like _bl_ue.**

 START!

| | | | | | |
|---|---|---|---|---|---|
| (bl<u>ue</u>) | eq<u>u</u>als | sn<u>ow</u> | j<u>u</u>mp | t<u>oa</u>st | s<u>au</u>sage |
| t<u>u</u>rn | J<u>u</u>ne | r<u>u</u>n | g<u>oa</u>t | exc<u>u</u>se | pl<u>u</u>s |
| yell<u>ow</u> | m<u>ou</u>th | sh<u>oo</u>ts | ch<u>ew</u> | d<u>u</u>ck | r<u>oo</u>m |

FINISH!

# What time is it around the world?

**1** **Look and answer the questions.**

**1** What time is it in Buenos Aires?

It's _eight o'clock_ in the morning.

**2** What time is it in London?

It's _____ in the afternoon.

**3** What time is it in Dubai?

It's _____ .

**4** What time is it in Shanghai?

It's _____ .

**2** **Draw a picture and write sentences.**

**1** I _____ at eight o'clock in

the morning.

**2** I _____

_____ .

**3** I _____

_____ .

**4** I _____

_____ .

# Evaluation

## 1 Look and complete the questions and answers.

**1** What time do you get up?

*I get up at six thirty.*

**2** What time do you get dressed?

_____

**3** _____

I go to school at eight o'clock.

**4** _____

I have dinner at seven thirty.

**5** What time do you brush your teeth?

_____

**6** _____

I go to bed at nine o'clock.

## 2 (About Me) Look at activity 1. Write sentences. Start with *So do I* or *I don't*.

1  *So do I. I get up at six thirty.*

2  _____

3  _____

4  _____

5  _____

6  _____

## 3 (About Me) Complete the sentences about this unit.

1  I can talk about _____ .

2  I can write about _____ .

3  My favorite part is _____ .

## 4 (Puzzle) Guess what it is.

Go to page 93 and circle the answer.

45

# Review Units 3 and 4

**1** **Look and complete the sentences about my day.**

> after lunch   after school   at four o'clock
> at nine o'clock.   at six thirty   at ten o'clock

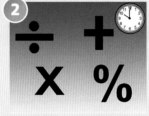

1  I go to school _at nine o'clock_ .   2  We have math _____ .

3  We have art _____ .   4  We have tennis club _____ .

5  I go home _____ .   6  I have dinner _____ .

**2** **About Me** **Write questions and answers.**

> ~~get up~~   go to bed   have breakfast | ~~on Monday~~   on Saturday   on Sunday

1  _What time do you get up on Monday?_ _____

_I get up_ _____

2  _____

_____

3  _____

_____

## 3 Find the words ↓ →. Use the words to complete the verbs.

**1**

get _dressed_

**2**

take a _____

| | | | | | | | |
|---|---|---|---|---|---|---|---|
| B | H | F | D | T | E | E | T | H |
| R | W | V | I | P | K | E | X | M |
| E | L | U | N | C | H | L | U | S |
| A | O | Y | N | C | G | B | A | C |
| K | D | R | E | S | S | E | D | H |
| F | M | E | R | B | O | D | C | O |
| A | Z | R | W | E | G | H | H | O |
| S | H | O | W | E | R | Q | R | L |
| T | X | L | B | A | U | P | C | Z |

**3**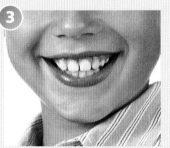

brush your _____

**4**

have _____

**5**

go to _____

**6**

have _____

**7**

have _____

**8**

go to _____

## 4  Answer the questions.

1   What day starts with the letter *M*?     _Monday_

2   What day has nine letters?     _____

3   What day comes after Thursday?     _____

4   What day comes before Sunday?     _____

5   What day has the letter *H* in it?     _____

6   What day sounds like M<u>o</u>nday?     _____

7   Put these letters in order: YADSUTE.     _____

47

# 5 Home time

## 1 Look and match.

a listen to music

b eat a sandwich

c do the dishes

d read a book

e drink juice

f make a cake

g watch TV

h wash the car

## 2 Look at activity 1. Complete the sentences.

1 Look at picture 1.    He's _reading a book_ .

2 Look at picture 2.    He's _____ .

3 Look at picture 4.    She's _____ .

4 Look at picture 6.    She's _____ .

5 Look at picture 7.    He's _____ .

## 3 (About Me) Answer the questions.

1 Do you like listening to music? _____

2 Do you like playing on the computer? _____

3 Do you like doing homework? _____

My picture dictionary  ➡ Go to page 89: Find and write the new words.

## 4 Read and match.

1 I love making cakes.

2 My mom likes listening to music.

3 My sister enjoys doing homework.

4 My brother doesn't enjoy playing this game on the computer.

5 My dad doesn't like doing the dishes.

## 5 Think Look and complete the sentences.

| like   love   doesn't enjoy   doesn't like | drink   read   wash   watch |

He _doesn't like drinking_ juice.

She _____ books.

He _____ TV.

She _____ the car.

## 6 About Me Write about your friend.

**Name:** _My friend's name_

1 _____ loves _____ .

2 _____ likes _____ .

3 _____ doesn't enjoy _____ .

## 7 Look and complete the questions. Then circle the answers.

1 Does he like _____reading books_____ ? (Yes, he does.) / No, he doesn't.

2 Does she enjoy _____ ? Yes, she does. / No, she doesn't.

3 Does she like _____ ? Yes, she does. / No, she doesn't.

4 Does he like _____ ? Yes, he does. / No, he doesn't.

5 Does he enjoy _____ ? Yes, he does. / No, he doesn't.

6 Does she like _____ ? Yes, she does. / No, she doesn't.

## 8 (Think) Look and complete the questions and answers. Then draw.

Does she enjoy ___making___ a cake?

No, ___she doesn't___ .

_____ enjoy_____ TV?

No, _____ .

_____ love _____

on the computer?

Yes, _____ .

_____ like _____

homework?

Yes, _____ .

## Skills: *Writing*

**9** **Read the paragraph and write the words.**

| love eating   enjoy cleaning   don't like doing   enjoy washing   ~~like making~~ |

I'm helpful at home. In the morning, I ¹___*like making*___ cakes, and I
²_____ them! I ³_____ my bedroom, too. In the
afternoon, I'm helpful. I ⁴_____ the dog or the car. After dinner,
I'm not helpful. I ⁵_____ the dishes!

**10** (About Me) **Answer the questions.**

**1** What do you enjoy cleaning?
_ I enjoy _____

**2** What do you like washing?
_____

**3** What do you like making?
_____

**4** What do you love doing?
_____

**5** What don't you like doing?
_____

**11** (About Me) **Write about being helpful at home.**

_I'm helpful at home. I like _____
_____
_____
_____
_____

**12** (About Me) **Ask and answer with a friend.**

Do you like cleaning your bedroom?          Yes, I do.

**13** **Read and write the words.**

> need   Watch out   so sorry   ~~likes making~~

**a** My Aunt Pat _likes making_ cakes.

Find a chocolate cake.

Great! Let's go to her house!

**b** What do we _____ ?

Eggs, milk, chocolate …

**c** _____ , Lucas!

Oh, no!

**d** Oh, dear! I'm _____ .

Me, too!

**14** **Look at activity 13. Answer the questions.**

1   Where are the children going?                     _Aunt Pat's house._

2   Does Aunt Pat like making cakes?                 _____

3   What do they need to make the cake?              _____

4   What does Lucas drop?                            _____

5   Who's sorry?                                     _____

**15** Look and check the picture that shows the value: show forgiveness.

**16** Color the words that sound like *tee**th***. Then answer the question.

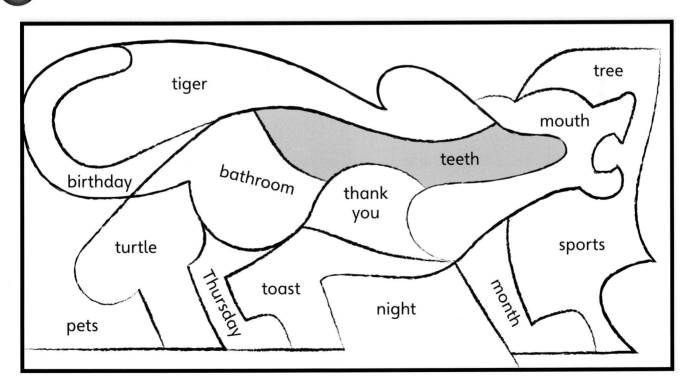

**What's this animal?** _____

# Where do people live?

**1** Find the words and write under the pictures.

> ~~wont~~  llivgea  ytic  ouidecyrtns

town

**2** Look and complete the sentences.

> café  houses  riding  stores  supermarket  town  ~~village~~  walking

In the [1] _village_ there
is a small [2]_____ . There
are two [3]_____ . People
like [4]_____ their bikes there.

In the [5]_____ , there are a lot
of [6]_____ and some stores.
You can buy food at the
[7]_____ . A lot of people
are [8]_____ in the street.

# Evaluation

## 1 Read and match. Then answer the questions.

Tom

a

c

e

1 read a book
2 do the dishes
3 do homework
4 listen to music
5 make a cake
6 drink juice

Cara

b

d

f

1 Does she like reading a book?     _Yes, she does._

2 Does she love doing the dishes?   _____

3 Does he like doing homework?      _____

4 Does he enjoy drinking juice?     _____

## 2 Look at activity 1. Complete the sentences.

1 Tom enjoys _doing homework_ .

2 Tom loves _____ , but he doesn't like _____ .

3 Cara loves _____ .

4 Cara doesn't enjoy _____ , but she likes _____ .

## 3  Complete the sentences about this unit.

1 I can talk about _____ .

2 I can write about _____ .

3 My favorite part is _____ .

## 4   Guess what it is.

Go to page 93 and circle the answer.

# 6 Hobbies

## 1 Look and number the picture.

1 play volleyball
2 make movies
3 do gymnastics
4 play the guitar
5 play Ping-Pong
6 play the recorder

## 2 Look and write the words.

| make do ~~play~~ play | models ~~badminton~~ the piano karate |

1  _play_
   _badminton_

2  _____
   _____

3  _____
   _____

4  _____
   _____

## 3 Think Write the words from activities 1 and 2 on the lists.

| Crafts | Music | Sports |
|--------|-------|--------|
| _make movies_ | | |
| | | |
| | | |
| | | |
| | | |

**My picture dictionary** ➔ Go to page 90: Find and write the new words.

**Look and follow. Then write *true* or *false*.**

| Dan | Anna | Jon | Jamie | May |

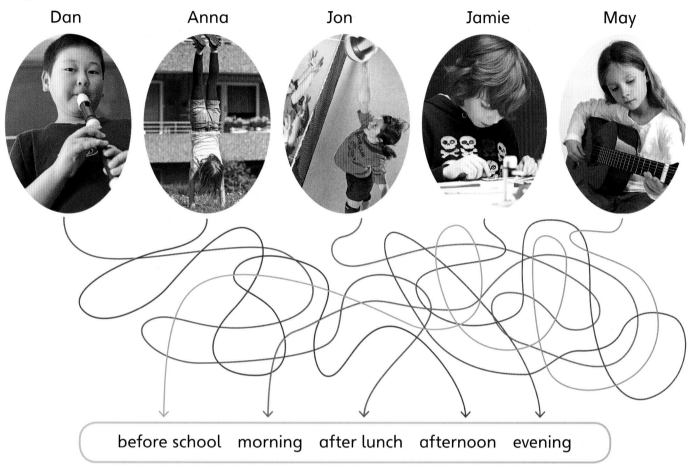

before school   morning   after lunch   afternoon   evening

**1** Dan plays the recorder before school.    *false*

**2** Anna does gymnastics in the afternoon.    _____

**3** Jon plays volleyball in the evening.    _____

**4** Jamie makes models in the morning.    _____

**5** May plays the guitar before school.    _____

 **Look at activity 4. Complete the sentences.**

**1** Dan *doesn't play the recorder* before school.

**2** Anna _____ in the afternoon.

**3** Jon _____ in the evening.

**4** Jamie _____ in the morning.

**5** May _____ before school.

**6** **Look and read. Then answer the questions.**

Hi, Jack. Baseball game on Saturday morning.

Jack, remember model club is Tuesday afternoon. Ben

Hello, Jack. Don't forget gymnastics club Tuesday morning before school. Mom

Ella, see you Thursday evening for your piano lesson.

Hi, Ella. Don't forget movie club is Friday evening! Amy

Ella. Remember karate club Sunday morning. Dad

1 Does Jack play baseball on Saturdays? _____Yes, he does._____

2 Does Ella play piano in the afternoon? _____

3 Does Jack make models in the evening? _____

4 Does Ella make movies on Sundays? _____

5 Does Jack do gymnastics before school? _____

6 Does Ella do karate on Sundays? _____

**7**   **Write questions about Jack and Ella.**

do gymnastics   make movies   make models
~~play the guitar~~   play the piano   play volleyball

1 ___Does___ Jack _play the guitar_ on Saturdays? No, he doesn't.

2 _____ Ella _____ on Thursdays? Yes, she does.

3 _____ Jack _____ on Tuesdays? Yes, he does.

4 _____ Ella _____ in the evening? Yes, she does.

5 _____ Jack _____ in the morning? Yes, he does.

6 _____ Ella _____ on Sundays? No, she doesn't.

## Skills: *Writing*

**8** **Read the paragraph and write the words.**

> after school   competitions   drink   hungry   ~~swimming~~   afternoon

My favorite sport is ¹ <u>swimming</u> . I swim every Saturday and Sunday
² _____ . Sometimes there are ³_____ . I'm always ⁴_____
after swimming! I eat a sandwich and ⁵_____ a glass of milk.
I enjoy playing tennis, too. We play ⁶_____ on Friday.

**9** (About Me) **Answer the questions.**

**1** What is your favorite sport?

  *My favorite sport is* _____

**2** When do you do it?

  _____

**3** Are there any competitions?

  _____

**4** What do you eat and drink after playing sports?

  _____

**10** (About Me) **Write about your favorite sport.**

  *My favorite sport* _____

  _____

  _____

  _____

  _____

  _____

**11** (About Me) **Ask and answer with a friend.**

> What's your favorite sport?    My favorite sport is horseback riding.

## 12 Read and number in order.

a — Good job, Lucas!
This is fun!

b — Hi, Lily. Come and play the guitar with me!
OK, great!

c — Where can we get a guitar?
Let's ask my cousin, Kim. She plays in a band.
1

d — Here, Lucas. Do you want to play the guitar, too?
No, I'm sorry. I can't play!
Come on, Lucas! Try it.

e — Practice every day, Lucas.

f — You can do it, Lucas! Like this …
Oh, dear!

## 13 Look at activity 12. Circle the answers.

**1** Who plays in a band?
  a Tom's cousin    b Lily's cousin (circled)    c Lily

**2** Who wants to play guitar with Kim?
  a Lily    b Anna    c Tom

**3** What can't Lucas do?
  a play in a band    b find a guitar    c play the guitar

**4** What is fun for Lucas?
  a watching Kim    b trying new things    c playing in a band

**5** What does Kim want Lucas to do every day?
  a practice the guitar    b play in Kim's band    c try new things

**14** Look and check the pictures that show the value: try new things.

**15** Circle the words that sound like *shark*.

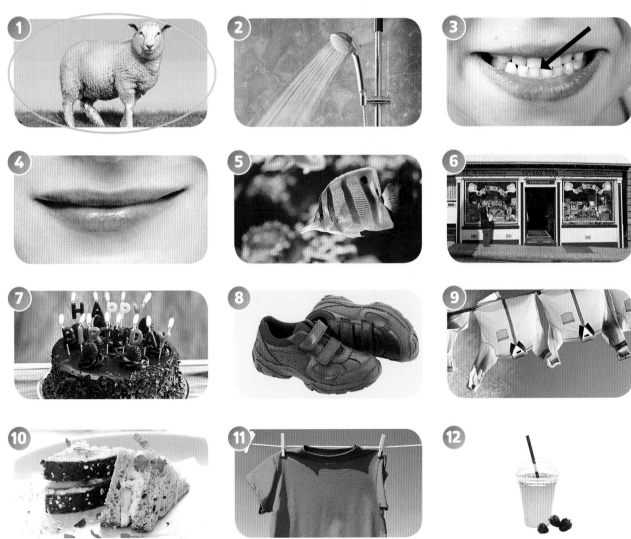

# What type of musical instrument is it?

**1** Look and guess. Then find and write the words.

girstn   srabs   sserciupon   ~~wwddinoo~~

woodwind

**2** Complete the sentences.

1 The drum _____ is a percussion instrument _____ .

2 The guitar _____ .

3 The piano _____ .

4 The recorder _____ .

**3** About Me **Ask and answer with a friend.**

What instrument do you like?       I like the piano!

# Evaluation

**1** **Look and complete the Venn diagram. Then answer the questions.**

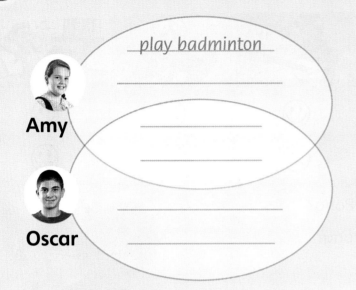

*play badminton*

Amy

Oscar

| Day | Amy | Oscar |
|---|---|---|
| Monday morning | | |
| Tuesday after school | | |
| Thursday afternoon | | |
| Friday evening | | |

**1** Does Amy play the piano on Tuesdays? *Yes, she does.*

**2** Does Oscar play the piano on Tuesdays? _____

**3** Does Amy do karate on Fridays? _____

**4** Does Oscar do karate on Tuesdays? _____

**2** **Look at activity 1. Complete the sentences about Oscar.**

**1** _He doesn't play_ Ping-Pong after school.

**2** _____ gymnastics on Wednesdays.

**3** _____ karate in the morning.

**4** _____ the piano on Fridays.

**3** (About Me) **Complete the sentences about this unit.**

**1** I can talk about _____ .

**2** I can write about _____ .

**3** My favorite part is _____ .

**4** Puzzle **Guess what it is.**

Go to page 93 and circle the answer.

# Review  Units 5 and 6

**1** **Look and answer the questions.**

| | | | | |
|---|---|---|---|---|
| Jade | ☹ | ☺ | ☺ | ☺ |
| Ben | ☺ | ☹ | ☹ | ☺ |

1  Does Ben enjoy playing Ping-Pong?  _Yes, he does._

2  Does Jade like playing Ping-Pong?  _____

3  Does Ben like reading?  _____

4  Does Jade love listening to music?  _____

5  Does Ben enjoy playing the guitar?  _____

6  Does Jade love playing the guitar?  _____

Ben    Jade

**2** **Look at activity 1. Complete the sentences.**

1  Jade loves  _listening to music_ , but she doesn't like _____ .

2  Ben enjoys _____ , but he doesn't like _____ .

3  Jade likes _____ , but she loves _____ .

4  Ben loves _____ , but he doesn't like _____ .

**3**  (About Me)  **Answer the questions.**

1  Do you like playing Ping-Pong?

_____

2  Do you like playing the guitar?

_____

3  Do you like making lunch?

_____

4  Do you like washing clothes?

_____

**4** Look and write the verbs on the lists.

**do**

**1** *do your homework*

**2** _____

**3** _____

**make**

**4** _____

**5** _____

**6** _____

**play**

**7** _____

**8** _____

**9** _____

**5** Look at activity 4. Write sentences.

**1** I _____ in the afternoon.

**2** I _____ on Saturdays.

**3** I like _____ , but _____ .

**4** I enjoy _____ , but _____ .

# 7 At the market

**1** (Think) **Look and do the word puzzle.**

Across →

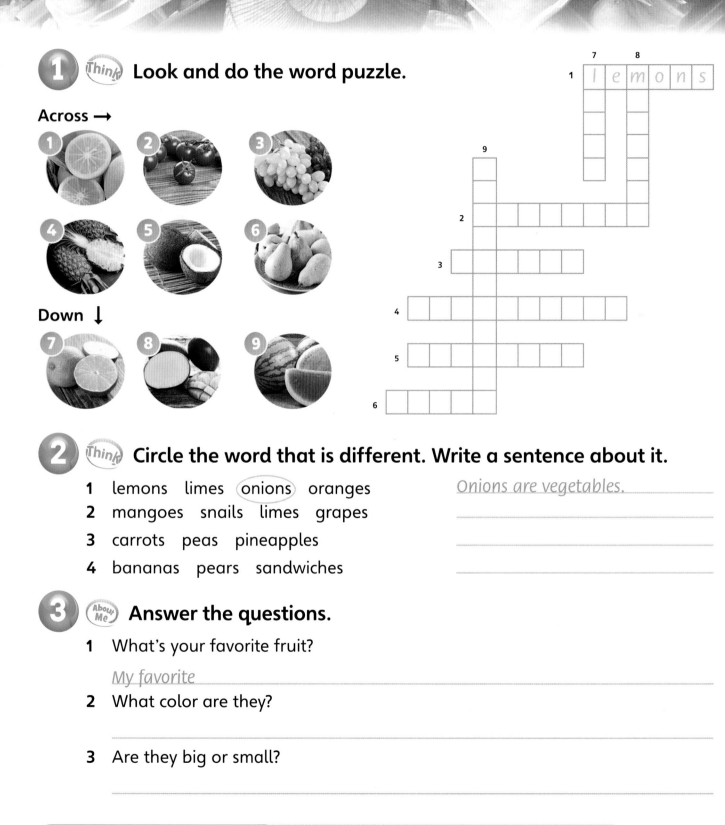

Down ↓

**2** (Think) **Circle the word that is different. Write a sentence about it.**

1  lemons   limes   (onions)   oranges        _Onions are vegetables._

2  mangoes   snails   limes   grapes        _____

3  carrots   peas   pineapples        _____

4  bananas   pears   sandwiches        _____

**3** (About Me) **Answer the questions.**

1  What's your favorite fruit?

   _My favorite_ _____

2  What color are they?

   _____

3  Are they big or small?

   _____

 **My picture dictionary** → **Go to page 91 : Find and write the new words.**

## 4 Read and circle the correct pictures.

**1** There are lots of pineapples.

**2** There are some onions.

**3** There aren't any tomatoes.

**4** There are lots of mangoes.

## 5  Look and complete the sentences with *lots of*, *some*, or *not any*.

**1** There _____*aren't any*_____ onions.

**2** There _____ vegetables.

**3** There _____ bananas.

**4** There _____ tomatoes.

**5** There _____ carrots.

**6** Look and check *yes* or *no.*

|  | Yes, there are. | No, there aren't. |
|---|---|---|
| **1** Are there any apples? | ☐ | ✔ |
| **2** Are there any carrots? | ☐ | ☐ |
| **3** Are there any mangoes? | ☐ | ☐ |
| **4** Are there any beans? | ☐ | ☐ |
| **5** Are there any watermelons? | ☐ | ☐ |

**7** Look at activity 6. Complete the questions and answers.

1 _____Are there any_____ grapes?  _____Yes, there are._____

2 _____ coconuts?  _____

3 _____ lemons?  _____

4 _____ pineapples?  _____

## Skills: *Writing*

**8** **Read the paragraph and write the words.**

any   aren't   ~~favorite~~   juice   like   some

My ¹ _favorite_ smoothie is Tropical Yum. I like orange ² _____ .
It's in my favorite smoothie. Bananas are my favorite fruit. There are
³ _____ bananas in my smoothie. There aren't ⁴ _____ limes.
I don't ⁵ _____ them. They ⁶ _____ sweet.

**9** (About Me) **Answer the questions.**

1 What's your favorite smoothie? Can you think of a name for it?

_My favorite smoothie is_ _____

2 Which juice do you like? Is it in your smoothie?

_____

3 Make a list of the fruit in your smoothie.

_____

4 What fruit don't you like in your smoothie?

_____

**10** (About Me) **Write about your favorite smoothie.**

_My favorite smoothie_ _____

_____

_____

_____

_____

_____

**11** (About Me) **Ask and answer with a friend.**

What's your favorite smoothie?        My favorite smoothie is ...

**Read and write the words.**

are   has   ~~lots of~~   red one   don't have

a

There are _lots of_ purses.

We _____ any money.

b

There _____ lots of old clothes in here.

Great! Let's look for a purse!

c

Yes! Look!

She _____ two purses!

d

Which purse do you want?

The _____ .

**Look at activity 12. Circle the answers.**

1   They're looking for a _____ .
   a   (purse)         b   guitar        c   hat

2   They don't have any _____ .
   a   shoes           b   old clothes   c   money

3   There are lots of _____ .
   a   new clothes     b   big clothes   c   old clothes

4   Anna has _____ .
   a   an old purse    b   two purses    c   two red purses

5   Lily wants the _____ .
   a   blue purse      b   red purse     c   new purse

**14** Look and check the pictures that show the value: reuse old things.

**15** Draw the shapes around the words with the same sound.

☐ = sh ◯ = ch

# What parts of plants can we eat?

**1** **Look and guess. Then find and write the words.**

~~pragse~~   nabasan   sepa   insono   torcars

**1**

grapes

**2**

_____

**3**

_____

**4**

_____

**5**

_____

**2** **Look at activity 1. Read and complete the sentences.**

1   They're seeds. They're small. They're green. They're _____ peas _____ .

2   They're roots. They're orange. Rabbits like eating them. They're _____ .

3   They're purple fruit. We can't buy one. We buy lots of them. They're _____ .

4   They're stems. They're long. We don't eat them for breakfast. They're _____

5   They're yellow fruit. Monkeys enjoy eating them. They're _____ .

# Evaluation

**1**  **Color the fruits and vegetables. Then answer the questions.**

| | | |
|---|---|---|
| **1** | Are there any apples? | Yes, there are. |
| **2** | Are there any grapes? | |
| **3** | Are there any pears? | |
| **4** | Are there any watermelons? | |
| **5** | Are there any carrots? | |
| **6** | Are there any pineapples? | |

**2**  **Write about your classroom.**

> pencils   desks   flowers   ~~books~~   rabbits   windows

**1** There are lots of ___books___ .          **2** There are some _____ .

**3** _____          **4** _____

**5** There aren't any _____ .          **6** _____

**3**  **Complete the sentences about this unit.**

**1** I can talk about _____ .

**2** I can write about _____ .

**3** My favorite part is _____ .

**4**  **Guess what it is.**

> Go to page 93 and circle the answer.

# 8 At the beach

## 1 Look and write the words. Then color the picture.

1 Color the _sun_ yellow.

2 Next to the towel is a _____ . Color it pink.

3 On the towel are some red and white _____ .

4 Can you see some _____ ? Color them blue.

## 2 Find and circle. Then match and write the words.

friesswimsuitoceantowelsandburger

_fries_

My picture dictionary ➔ Go to page 92: Find and write the new words.

**3** (Think) **Look and write the words.**

hers   his   mine   ours   ~~theirs~~   yours

**1** Which umbrella is ___theirs___ ? The red one.

**2** Which umbrella is _____ ? The purple one.

**3** Which sock is _____ ? The white one.

**4** Which sock is _____ ? The yellow one.

**5** Which hat is _____ ?

**6** The green one's _____ .

**4** **Look and answer the questions.**

**1** Which shell is his?          _The yellow one's his._

**2** Which shell is hers?         _____

**3** Which towel is theirs?       _____

**4** Which towel is ours?         _____

**5** Which rabbit is mine?        _____

**5** **Think** Look and circle the words.

Whose jacket is (that) / this?
(It's) / They're Ana's.

Whose shoes are **these** / **those**?
It's / **They're** theirs.

Whose bags are **these** / **those**?
It's / **They're** yours.

Whose sunglasses are **these** / **those**?
It's / **They're** mine.

Whose house is **this** / **that**?
It's / **They're** ours.

**6** Look and complete the questions and answers.

_Whose_ hat _is this_ ?
_It's_ his.

_____ bike _____ ?
_____ Tim's.

_____ paintings _____ ?
_____ mine.

_____ pencils _____ ?
_____ theirs.

# Skills: *Writing*

**7** **Read the postcard and answer the questions.**

**1** Where is Dylan?

At the beach.

**2** What does he like doing in the morning?

_____

**3** Who does he enjoy playing with?

_____

**4** What does he do in the afternoon?

_____

**5** What does he eat for lunch?

_____

> Dear Renata,
>
>   We are having a great vacation. We're at the beach.
>
>   I like flying my kite in the morning. I enjoy playing with my sister. In the afternoon, I swim in the ocean. It's great. There are lots of people swimming in the ocean. But there aren't any sharks. ☺
>
>   At lunchtime, we go to the café. I eat sausages and fries.
>
> See you soon,
> Dylan

**8** (About Me) **Imagine you're on vacation. Answer the questions.**

**1** Where are you?    I'm _____

**2** Who is on vacation with you? _____

**3** What do you do in the morning? _____

**4** What do you do in the afternoon? _____

**5** What do you eat? _____

**9** (About Me) **Write a postcard to a friend.**

Dear _____

I'm having a _____

_____

_____

_____

_____

**10** (About Me) **Ask and answer with a friend.**

What do you do on vacation?    I swim in the ocean.

**11** **Read and match.**

| | |
|---|---|
| **1** Hi. Do you have my seven things? | **2** Good idea. Let's ask my dad. |
| **3** We hope you enjoy it! | **4** Thank you, Mr. Lin. |

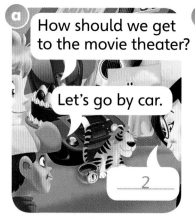

**a** How should we get to the movie theater?

Let's go by car.

___2___

**b** Wait a minute! Whose car is that?

It's Aunt Pat's.

**c** Aunt Pat!

**d** Welcome to our show!

**12** **Look at activity 11. Circle the answers.**

**1** Where do they go?
   **a** to the supermarket    **b** to the school    **c** to the movie theater

**2** How do they get there?
   **a** by bike             **b** by car          **c** by bus

**3** How many things do they have?
   **a** three             **b** five             **c** seven

**4** Whose things are they?
   **a** Lily's             **b** Aunt Pat's    **c** Mr. Lin's

**5** What are the things for?
   **a** family and friends    **b** Anna         **c** a show

**13** Look and write the answers. Then check the picture that shows the value: appreciate your family and friends.

> Thank you!   ~~Dinner is ready!~~   Five minutes, Mom!   You're a great dad!

*Dinner is ready!*

**14** Circle the words that sound like *dol**ph**in*.

# Are sea animals symmetrical?

**1** **Look and write the words.**

jellyfish   octopus   crab   ~~shell~~   sea horse   starfish

shell

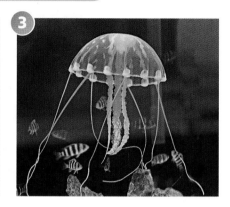

**2** **Look at activity 1. Write about the sea animals.**

1  This shell is small. In this picture, the shell is symmetrical.

2  _____

3  _____

4  _____

5  _____

6  _____

# Evaluation

## 1 Look and do the word puzzle.

**Across**

**Down**

## 2 Think Look and circle the answers.

1  Whose backpack is this? It's **hers** / **his.**

3  Which hat is his? **It's the white one.** / **It's the red one.**

2  Whose ball is this? It's **his** / **hers.**

4  Which jacket is hers? **It's the green one.** / **It's the blue one.**

## 3 About Me Complete the sentences about this unit.

1  I can talk about ——————— .

2  I can write about ——————— .

3  My favorite part is ——————— .

## 4 Puzzle Guess what it is.

Go to page 93 and circle the answer.

# Review Units 7 and 8

**1** **Look and answer the questions.**

| | | |
|---|---|---|
| **1** | Are there any shorts? | *Yes, there are.* |
| **2** | Are there any sunglasses? | |
| **3** | Are there any shells? | |
| **4** | Is there a swimsuit? | |
| **5** | Is there a towel? | |
| **6** | Are there any pineapples? | |
| **7** | Are there any lemons? | |
| **8** | Is there a watermelon? | |
| **9** | Are there any onions? | |
| **10** | Are there any coconuts? | |

**2** Think **Look and match. Complete the sentences with *some*, *lots of*, or *not any*.**

**1** *There are some* tomatoes.
**2** _____ pears.
**3** _____ lemons.
**4** _____ shells.
**5** _____ grapes.
**6** _____ fries.

## 3 Look and circle the words.

**1** Whose pineapple is **this** / **that**?

*(this is circled)*

**It's** / **They're** yours.

*(It's is circled)*

**2** Whose onions are **these** / **those**?

**It's** / **They're** yours.

**3** Whose limes are **these** / **those**?

**It's** / **They're** mine.

**4** Whose shell is **this** / **that**?

**It's** / **They're** mine.

## 4  Look and circle the words. Then answer the questions.

**1** Which camera is **hers** / **yours**?

*(yours is circled)*

*The small one's mine.*

**2** Which kite is **his** / **yours**?

_____

**3** Which pencil case is **his** / **ours**?

_____

**4** Which towel is **his** / **theirs**?

_____

**5** Which bag is **hers** / **his**?

_____

# Welcome

Lucas   Anna   Max   Tom   Lily

March   December   January   August   April   October
June   November   May   February   July   September

| J _ _ _ _ | F _ _ _ _ | M _ _ _ |
| A _ _ _ | M _ _ | J _ _ _ |
| J _ _ | A _ _ _ | S _ _ _ _ |
| O _ _ _ | N _ _ _ | D _ _ _ _ |

# (1) In the yard

snail    guinea pig    caterpillar    turtle    butterfly
tree    flower    grass    rabbit    leaf

_____    _____    _____    _____

_____    _____    _____    _____

_____    _____

# 2 At school

reception   library   sports field   classroom   gym   music room
cafeteria   art room   playground   science lab

# 3 School days

Saturday  Tuesday  Monday  Thursday
Sunday  Wednesday  Friday

M

T

W

T

F

S

S

# 4 My day

go to school    get up    take a shower    have breakfast    get dressed
have lunch    go home    have dinner    brush your teeth    go to bed

# 5 Home time

do homework   watch TV   do the dishes   listen to music   wash the car
play on the computer   drink juice   make a cake   read a book   eat a sandwich

# 6 Hobbies

play the recorder   play Ping-Pong   do karate   play badminton   make models
play the guitar   make movies   play the piano   do gymnastics   play volleyball

onions   coconuts   watermelons   mangoes   pineapples
tomatoes   limes   pears   lemons   grapes

swimsuit   fries   shells   sun   burger   sunglasses   sand   towel   ocean   shorts

**1** **Find the words ↓ →. Use the colored letters to answer the question.**

| P | G | L | I | B | R | A | R | Y | A | R | C | U | B |
|---|---|---|---|---|---|---|---|---|---|---|---|---|---|
| I | Q | E | R | T | G | Y | J | K | E | L | P | V | E |
| N | L | A | B | U | T | T | E | R | F | L | Y | U | V |
| E | B | Z | M | S | W | L | H | B | G | T | D | A | M |
| A | M | N | F | O | T | D | W | B | I | I | S | O | A |
| P | G | O | A | O | S | H | O | W | E | R | H | X | T |
| P | A | A | N | M | G | I | R | C | M | Q | E | Z | H |
| L | S | G | N | H | K | L | U | Y | O | O | L | P | M |
| E | M | U | A | N | T | U | E | R | N | S | L | L | Y |
| X | V | I | E | B | G | H | Y | O | P | W | F | R | Y |
| D | O | T | H | E | D | I | S | H | E | S | O | K | R |
| J | K | A | S | K | V | B | Y | U | W | E | T | R | E |
| M | I | R | W | T | E | C | J | F | H | A | N | N | A |

**Q:** What are two things people can't eat before breakfast?

**A:** _ _ _ _ _ and _ _ _ _ _ _

# Story fun

**1** Match the objects to the words. Then match the words to the story units they come from.

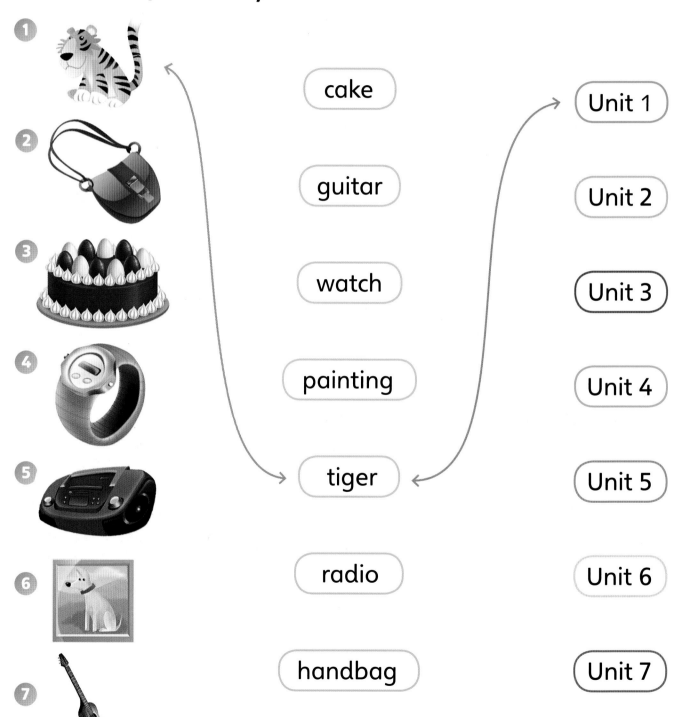

cake

guitar

watch

painting

tiger

radio

handbag

Unit 1

Unit 2

Unit 3

Unit 4

Unit 5

Unit 6

Unit 7

# 1. Write the numbers in the box of the objects in Aunt Pat's show.

# Thanks and Acknowledgments

The authors and publishers would like to thank the following contributors:

**Blooberry Design:** concept design, book design, page make-up
**Fiona Davis:** editing
**Lisa Hutchins:** freelance editing
**John Marshall Media:** audio recording and production
**hyphen S.A.:** publishing management, American English edition

The authors and publishers acknowledge the following sources of copyright material and are grateful for the permissions granted. Although every effort has been made, it has not always been possible to identify the sources of all the material used or to trace all copyright holders. If any omissions are brought to our notice, we will be happy to include the appropriate acknowledgments on reprinting.

**The authors and publishers would like to thank the following illustrators:**

Pablo Gallego (Beehive Illustration): pp. 3, 4, 8, 11, 16, 24, 34, 42, 52, 60, 70, 78, 84; Gareth Conway (Bright Agency): pp. 9, 14, 38, 50, 75, 83; Brian Lee: pp. 10, 18, 54; Humberto Blanco (Sylvie Poggio): pp. 13, 21, 27, 45, 50, 56, 82; Simon Walmesley: pp. 13, 14, 22, 28, 39, 64, 68, 74, 75, 83; A Corazon Abierto (Sylvie Poggio): pp. 17, 48, 53, 65, 71, 79; Ilias Arahovitis (Beehive Illustration): pp. 19, 20, 26, 30, 31, 37, 55, 67, 73; Luke Newell: pp. 19, 35, 49, 76; Marcus Cutler (Sylvie Poggio): pp. 25, 35, 53, 61; Graham Kennedy: pp. 29, 36, 46, 76; Mark Duffin: pp. 22, 44; Monkey Feet: pp. 85, 86, 88, 89, 90, 91, 92.

**The authors and publishers would like to thank the following for permission to reproduce photographs:**

p. 4 (unit header): © TongRo Images/Alamy; p. 5: pirita/Shutterstock; p. 7 (B/G): KPG_Payless/Shutterstock; p. 7 (TR): © Rob Walls/Alamy; p. 10 (unit header): © Martyn Goddard/Alamy; p. 10 (wood frames): homydesign/Shutterstock; p.10 (gold frames): worker/Shutterstock; p. 12 (unit header): © David Wong/Getty; p. 12 (photo 1): Premaphotos/Alamy; (photo 2): Johan Larson/Shutterstock; (photo 3): sevenke/Shutterstock; (photo 4): Roman Sigaev/Shutterstock; (photo 5): Alexander Mak/Shutterstock; (photo 6): E. Spek/Shutterstock; (photo 7): hramovnick/Shutterstock; (photo 8): vaklav/Shutterstock; (photo 9): Perutskyi Petro/Shutterstock; (photo 10): Jaroslav74/Shutterstock; p. 15 (B/G): liubomir/Shutterstock; p. 18 (unit header): Laszio Halasi/Shutterstock; p. 19 (BR): Vetapi/Shutterstock; p. 20 (unit header): © Kike Calvo/National Geographic Society/Corbis; p. 21 (photo 1): Amy Myers/Shutterstock; (photo 2): Monkey Business Images/Shutterstock; (photo 3): © Adrian Sherratt/Alamy; (photo 4): wavebreakmedia/Shutterstock; p. 23 (B/G): Mark Herreid/Shutterstock; p. 25 (photo 1): neelsky/Shutterstock; (photo 2): S-F/Shutterstock; (photo 3): Korionov/Shutterstock; (photo 4): Ti Santi/Shutterstock; (photo 5): Elena Elisseeva/Shutterstock; (photo 6): EBFoto/Shutterstock; (photo 7): TSpider/Shutterstock; (photo 8): dotshock/Shutterstock; (photo 9): stable/Shutterstock; p. 26 (unit header): Lightspring/Shutterstock; p. 27 (BR): Radu Bercan/Shutterstock; p. 29 (TR): Purestock/Alamy; (BR): © Cultura RM/Alamy; p. 30 (unit header): © Randy Plett/Getty; (TR): Joshua Hodge Photography/Getty; p. 32 (TR): © Heide Benser/Corbis; p. 33 (B/G): ThomasLENNE/Shutterstock; p. 36 (unit header): © Adam Jones/Visuals Unlimited/Corbis; p. 37 (TR): Stewart Cohen/Corbis; p. 38 (unit header): © Kristian Buus/Corbis; p. 40: David Ashley/Corbis; p. 41 (B/G): Shailth/Shutterstock; TR: Nino Mascardi/Getty; p. 45 (BR): Mile Atanasov/Shutterstock; p. 46 (TL): Hero Images Inc./Corbis; p. 47 (photo 1): JGI/Jamie Grill/Getty; (photo 2): Offscreen/Shutterstock; (photo 3): Roger Jegg/Shutterstock; (photo 4): D. Pimborough/Shutterstock; (photo 5): © Ian Miles/Flashpoint Pictures/Alamy; (photo 6): © Andrea Heselton/Alamy; (photo 7): tama2012/Shutterstock; (photo 8): © Arcaid Images/Alamy;

p. 48 (unit header): Adrian Cook/Alamy; p. 49 (photo a): p_ponomareva/Shutterstock; (photo b): Blend Images/Shutterstock; (photo c): Rido/Shutterstock; (photo d): MBI/Alamy; (photo e): © Deborah Vernon/Alamy; p. 51 (B/G): LanKS/Shutterstock; p. 54 (unit header): © Michael Marquand/Getty; (photo 1): antb/Shutterstock; (photo 2): Videowokart/Shutterstock; (photo 3): Boris Stroujko/Shutterstock; (photo 4): dbimages/Alamy; p. 55 (TL, ML, BL): Sergey Novikov/Shutterstock; (TR, MR, BR): Goodluz/Shutterstock; (BR): Joe Cox/Shutterstock; p. 56 (unit header): Tadej Zupancic/Getty; (photo 1): George Doyle/Getty; (photo 2): p_ponomareva/Shutterstock; (photo 3): © Mikhail Kondrashov/fotomik/Alamy; (photo 4): Monkey Business Images/Shutterstock; p. 57 (photo 1): amana images inc./Alamy; (photo 2): © Westend61 GmbH/Alamy; (photo 3): © Prisma Bildagentur AG/Alamy; (photo 4): © Kenny Williamson/Alamy; (photo 5): wentus/Shutterstock; p. 58 (TL, TM, TR): Sombat Kapan/Shutterstock; (BL, BM, BR): Bipsun/Shutterstock; p. 59 (B/G): nattanan726/Shutterstock; p. 61 (photo 1): Tom Bird/Shutterstock; (photo 2): lendy16/Shutterstock; (photo 3): mikute/Shutterstock; (photo 4): ntstudio/Shutterstock; (photo 5): Anna Lurye/Shutterstock; (photo 6): © T.M.O.Buildings/Alamy; (photo 7): Romiana Lee/Shutterstock; (photo 8): Rob Hyrons/Shutterstock; (photo 9): Radka Tesarova/Shutterstock; (photo 10): Wiktory/Shutterstock; (photo 11): Mike Flippo/Shutterstock; (photo 12): M. Unal Ozmen/Shutterstock; p. 62 (unit header): © Richard T. Nowitz/Corbis; (photo 1): Yenwen Lu/Getty; (photo 2): © redsnapper/Alamy; (photo 3): © Bob Daemmrich/Alamy; (photo 4): Maxim Tarasyugin/Shutterstock; p. 63 (photo 1): Tatiana Popova/Shutterstock; (photo 2): Mendelex/Shutterstock; (photo 3): Vereshchagin Dmitry/Shutterstock; (photo 4): Attl Tibor/Shutterstock; (photo 5): bogdan ionescu/Shutterstock; (photo 6): Erik Isakson/Getty; (photo 7): Attl Tibor/Shutterstock; (photo 8): Vereshchagin Dmitry/Shutterstock; (photo 9): cristovao/Shutterstock; (photo 10): eurobanks/Shutterstock; (photo 11): EKS design/Shutterstock; p. 64: Edith Held/Corbis; p. 66 (unit header): © Gonzalo Azumendi/Getty; (photo 1): Candus Camera/Shutterstock; (photo 2): Daniel M Ernst/Shutterstock; (photo 3): George Dolgikh/Shutterstock; (photo 4): sjk2012/Shutterstock; (photo 5): Mukesh Kumar/Shutterstock; (photo 6): Antonova Anna/Shutterstock; (photo 7): IngridHS/Shutterstock; (photo 8): Nataliya Arzamasova/Shutterstock; (photo 9): BrazilPhotos/Shutterstock; p. 67 (BR): Aleksandar Mijatovic/Shutterstock; p. 69 (B/G): Valeri Potapova/Shutterstock; p. 71 (photo 1): nodff/Shutterstock; (photo 2): yykkaa/Shutterstock; (photo 3): Matt9122/Shutterstock; (photo 4): CREATISTA/Shutterstock; (photo 5): Africa Studio/Shutterstock; (photo 6): GoodMood Photo/Shutterstock; p. 72 (unit header): © MIXA/Alamy; (photo 1): Fabio Bernardi/Shutterstock; (photo 2): bergamont/Shutterstock; (photo 3): Kuttelvaserova Stuchelova/Shutterstock; (photo 4): Kesu/Shutterstock; (photo 5): Jiri Hera/Shutterstock; p. 73 (BR): Kozub Vasyl/Shutterstock; p. 74 (unit header): © Abflo photo/Getty; (photo 1): © foodfolio/Alamy; (photo 2): Denis Tabler/Shutterstock; (photo 3): ankiro/Shutterstock; (photo 4): K. Miri Photography/Shutterstock; (photo 5): Slavica Stajic/Shutterstock; (photo 6): stockcreations/Shutterstock; p. 77 (B/G): silvae/Shutterstock; p. 79 (photo 1): Juergen Faelchle/Shutterstock; (photo 2): Maryna Kulchytska/Shutterstock; (photo 3): Kondrachov Vladimir/Shutterstock; (photo 4): Donovan van Staden/Shutterstock; (photo 5): jannoon028/Shutterstock; (photo 6): Studio 1231/Shutterstock; (photo 7): Andrey Armyagov/Shutterstock; (photo 8): Rocketclips, Inc./Shutterstock; (photo 9): Bloomua/Shutterstock; p. 80 (unit header): © Dave Fleetham/Design Pics/Corbis; (photo 1): Lucy Liu/Shutterstock; (photo 2): Evocation Images/Shutterstock; (photo 3): QiuJu Song/Shutterstock; (photo 4): Olga Desyatun/Shutterstock; (photo 5): Vittorio Bruno/Shutterstock; (photo 6): Cuson/Shutterstock; p. 81 (photo 1): Dan Fairchild Photography/Getty; (photo 2): Mirek Kijewski/Shutterstock; (photo 3): Songchai W/Shutterstock; (photo 4): Photodisc/Getty; (photo 5): pyzata/Shutterstock; (photo 6): OliverSved/Shutterstock; (photo 7): Littlehenrabi/Shutterstock; (photo 8): Elena Shashkina/Shutterstock; (photo 9): Cherry-Merry/Shutterstock; (photo 10): © Steve Skjold/Alamy; (BR): ZiZ7StockPhotos/Shutterstock; p. 82 (photo 1): Filip Fuxa/Shutterstock; (photo 2): Givaga/Shutterstock; (photo 3): Lessimol/Shutterstock; (photo 4): Tei Sinthipsomboon/Shutterstock; (photo 5): Dutourdumonde Photography/Shutterstock; (photo 6): Anna Biancoloto/Shutterstock; p. 93 (puzzle header): StepanPopov/Shutterstock.

Front Cover photo by Sylvestre Machado/Getty Images